Hurricanes

WITNESS TO DISASTER

"Within the eye of a hurricane...exists a place of powerful beauty: sunshine streams into the windows of the plane from a perfect circle of blue sky directly above... surrounding the plane on all sides is the blackness of the eyewall's thunderstorms and directly below...peeking through a few low clouds lies a violent ocean."

Christopher Landsea,
Science and Operations Officer, National Hurricane Center

Hurricanes

WITNESS TO DISASTER

NATIONAL GEOGRAPHIC

WASHINGTON, D.C.

Text copyright © 2007 Judith Bloom Fradin and Dennis Brindell Fradin

Published by the National Geographic Society.

Founded in 1888, the National Geographic Society is one of the largest nonprofit scientific and educational organizations in the world. It reaches more than 285 million people worldwide each month through its official journal, NATIONAL GEOGRAPHIC, and its four other magazines; the National Geographic Channel; television documentaries; radio programs; films; books; videos and DVDs; maps; and interactive media. National Geographic has funded more than 8,000 scientific research projects and supports an education program combating geographic illiteracy.

For more information, please call 1-800-NGS-LINE (647-5463) or write to the following address:
National Geographic Society
1145 17th Street N.W.
Washington, D.C. 20036-4688
U.S.A.

Visit us online at www.nationalgeographic.com/books

For information about special discounts for bulk purchases, please contact National Geographic Books Special Sales: ngspecsales@ngs.org

For rights or permissions inquiries, please contact National Geographic Books Subsidiary Rights: ngbookrights@ngs.org

Fradin, Judith Bloom.
Hurricanes / by Judy and Dennis Fradin.
   p. cm.
Includes bibliographical references.
ISBN 978-1-4262-0111-0 (hardcover)
ISBN 978-1-4262-0112-7 (lib. bdg.)
1. Hurricanes. I. Fradin, Dennis B. II. Title.
QC944.F73 2007
904'.5--dc22
                        2006103003

Hardcover ISBN: 978-1-4262-0111-0
Library Edition ISBN: 978-1-4262-0112-7
Printed in Mexico

Series design by Daniel Banks,
Project Design Company

The body text is set in Meridien
The display text is set in ITC Franklin Gothic

National Geographic Society
John M. Fahey, Jr., President and Chief Executive Officer
Gilbert M. Grosvenor, Chairman of the Board
Nina D. Hoffman, Executive Vice President; President, Book Publishing Group

Staff for This Book
Nancy Laties Feresten, Vice President, Editor-in-Chief of Children's Books
Amy Shields, Executive Editor
Bea Jackson, Director of Design and Illustration
David Seager, Art Director
Lori Epstein, Illustrations Editor
Jean Cantu, Illustrations Specialist
Carl Mehler, Director of Maps
Jennifer A. Thornton, Managing Editor
Priyanka Lamichhane, Assistant Editor
R. Gary Colbert, Production Director
Lewis R. Bassford, Production Manager
Maryclare Tracy, Nicole Elliott, Manufacturing Managers

Photo Credits
front, Jim Reed; back, NASA; 2-3, Getty Images; 5, Digital Vision; 6, Jim Reed / Corbis; 7, NOAA; 8, Allen Fredrickson/Reuters; 9, Vincent Laforet/Pool/Reuters/Corbis; 10, Brian Snyder/Reuters; 11, John McCusker/The Times Picayune; 12, NOAA; 14, Paris Barrera/epa/Corbis; 15, NOAA; 16, NOAA; 17, COMET® http://meted.ucar.edu/ of the University Corporation for Atmospheric Research (UCAR) pursuant to a Cooperative Agreements with the National Oceanic and Atmospheric Administration, U.S. Department of Commerce. ©1997-2007 University Corporation for Atmospheric Research. All Rights Reserved. 18, Kevork Djansezian/ Associated Press; 19, NOAA; 20, NOAA; 23, NOAA 25, NASA; 26, Bettmann / Corbis; 28, Bill Lane/ Richmond Times Dispatch; 29, Harry Koundakjian/ Associated Press; 30, Paul Chesley/Getty Images; 31, Reportage/Getty Images; 32, NOAA; 33, Henry Romero/ Reuters / Corbis; 35, Tom Salyer/ Reuters / Corbis; 36, Reuters/ NOAA / Corbis; 38, NOAA; 39, China News Photo/ Reuters / Corbis; 40-41, NASA; 43, Cheryl Gerber/ Associated Press; 44, Mario Tama/Getty Images; 46, Bob Shanley/ Palm Beach Post/ZUMA Press;

CONTENTS

CHAPTER 1

"It Was Scary on the Roof"

Hurricane Katrina

After Hurricane Katrina struck New Orleans, a group of people await rescue as oil-streaked floodwaters creep toward their roof.

A satellite image taken as Katrina slams into New Orleans.

Urgent Weather Message, National Weather Service, New Orleans, LA 4:13 P.M. CDT, Sunday, August 28, 2005:

"Extremely dangerous hurricane Katrina... devastating damage expected... uninhabitable..."

"W hen I awoke on August 28, 2005, I turned on the TV and saw the latest satellite picture of Katrina," recalls Jake Herty III, a National Weather Service technician who lived outside New Orleans, Louisiana. "It put the fear of God in me. I had never seen a more intense storm."

As she whirled toward land on that last Sunday in August, Hurricane Katrina was already a killer. Three days earlier, Katrina had ripped into the Florida coast near Miami, toppling trees, flooding streets, and killing 14 people. But Katrina's winds had been blowing at "only" 80 miles per hour when she struck Florida, making her the weakest type of hurricane, a Category One.

After crossing Florida's southern tip, Katrina emerged over the Gulf of Mexico. Feeding off the warm Gulf waters, Katrina intensified into a monstrous storm. By the time Mr. Herty and other Gulf Coast residents tuned in the news on that Sunday morning, Katrina had become a Category Five hurricane—the most powerful type. That day her winds were clocked at 175 miles per hour.

Her incredible power wasn't the only bad news about Katrina. On that

This levee protecting New Orleans was breached, which means the water broke through. The splash you see is from sandbags being dumped from a helicopter to try to fix the breach.

morning of August 28 the National Weather Service issued a bulletin predicting that Katrina was on target to slam into New Orleans. A major city with more than 1.3 million people in its metropolitan area, New Orleans was especially vulnerable to flooding because much of it lay below sea level. Water seeks its own level, and without a system of walls and pumps, parts of New Orleans would naturally be covered with water.

The mayor of New Orleans held a news conference. Calling Katrina the hurricane "that most of us have long feared," the mayor ordered the city evacuated. Most people obeyed the order. Since hurricanes generally do the most harm along and near the coast, more than a million people from the New Orleans area fled inland. Among them were Jake Herty III, his 82-year-old father, and their dog, Pepper. People in other communities along the Louisiana, Mississippi, and Alabama coasts joined in the exodus, for Katrina was more than 200 miles in diameter and was expected to wreak havoc far beyond the New Orleans region.

Hundreds of thousands of people stayed behind, however. Many of them lacked transportation. Others had nowhere to go or were too ill or frail to move.

At 6:10 A.M. on Monday, August 29, 2005, Katrina smashed into the Gulf Coast with winds howling at speeds exceeding 140 miles per hour. The hurricane also propelled storm surges—wind-driven walls of water—into coastal communities. Raging water and flying debris caused widespread damage and deaths in Alabama and Mississippi.

"The first water that flowed into New Orleans was clear, clean ocean water from the storm surges. But a few days later, the water turned black. It was incredibly smelly and dirty. The water was full of raw sewage and dead bodies. I developed a rash on my legs just from being in it."

Major Philip Kitchen, who rescued people by boat after Katrina struck

Photographer Mike Theiss captures the rush of Katrina's storm surge.

Hurricane Katrina's storm surges battered the levees (walls) designed to protect New Orleans from flooding. In some places the water flowed over the levees. Elsewhere it burst through these protective walls. By Tuesday, August 30, at least 80% of the city was underwater, as were communities near New Orleans.

With the water up to 25 feet deep, many people climbed onto rooftops to avoid drowning. "We got to the roof from the attic," recalls Lance Williams, a nine-year-old fourth grader who was forced onto a rooftop in New Orleans along with several relatives. "It was scary on the roof. All we could do was watch the water go by. There was a lot of thunder and lightning. But the scariest part was the wind. It started peeling the roof off the house. And it was slippery. I was afraid I was going to fall off. My uncle held my hand and we all hung on to each other."

Boats and helicopters were dispatched to evacuate survivors. Over the next few days tens of thousands of stranded people, including Lance Williams and his relatives, were rescued by the U.S. Coast Guard and other search-and-rescue teams.

"After Katrina hit, from 10 A.M. to 10 P.M. we rescued between 70 and 100 people by boat in gale-force winds," explains Major Philip Kitchen of the Orleans Parish Civil Sheriff's Office. The rescuers themselves were in danger of their boats sinking. "We had to move slowly and carefully, especially after dark, because there were cars, trees, and telephone poles beneath the water."

Katrina created other dangers besides water and wind, Major Kitchen says. "Gas lines were exposed, so there were fires and explosions. Houses were burning. Electric wires were down, too, so a number of people were electrocuted days after the hurricane."

Despite rescue efforts, Katrina claimed a huge toll in Louisiana. The monstrous hurricane killed about 1,600 people in the state, most of them in and near New Orleans.

WITNESS TO KATRINA

"After the water receded, I went back to New Orleans. Everything was covered with mold, and there was a terrible stench. Signs had been painted on houses saying SEARCHED and on some ONE DEAD or TWO DEAD."

Father Luis Aponte-Merced, a Catholic priest, describing the aftermath of Hurricane Katrina

Disasters create many heroes. John McCusker photographed these people rescuing small children in a rubber tub after breaks in the levees flooded parts of New Orleans.

After bashing the coast, Katrina continued northward, dropping heavy rains over a large inland region and still generating powerful winds. Jake Herty III, his dad, and their dog had taken refuge in a trailer home 50 miles north of New Orleans. "As the wind blew, for hours all we heard were pine trees snapping," Jake remembers. "It sounded just like rifle shots. The trailer got hit by limbs quite a few times. One huge pine tree came down on the trailer and tore open part of the roof." Fortunately, no one in the trailer was injured.

By the time Katrina disappeared over Canada late on August 31, she had been one of the deadliest hurricanes ever to strike the United States. Nearly 2,000 people were known to have been killed by the storm. Hundreds of others remain missing to this day. Katrina also destroyed many thousands of homes, forcing huge numbers of people to find new places to live. After being rescued off the rooftop by helicopter, Lance Williams moved with his family to Houston, Texas.

"In some of the hardest-hit places in New Orleans, lots of houses just aren't there anymore," explained Major Philip Kitchen, nearly a year after the disaster. "They were destroyed by the flood waters. You can go blocks and blocks and see no people—just a few pitiful cats and dogs. It will take at least 20 years to recover from this—assuming we're not hit again."

CHAPTER 2

"Never Did the Sky Look More Terrible"

The Science of Hurricanes

The Fujiwhara Effect is named after an early 20th century Japanese scientist. It describes tropical storms whirling in an atmospheric dance. They revolve around one another like two children holding hands and twirling in a circle. The twin hurricanes in this 1974 NOAA picture are Ione on the left and Kirsten on the right.

"Eyes never beheld the seas so high, angry, and covered by foam. Never did the sky look more terrible. The flashes of lightning came with such fury that we all thought the ships would be blasted. All this time the water never ceased to fall from the sky."

Christopher Columbus, describing a hurricane he encountered in 1503

Centuries ago the Mayans of Mexico and Central America believed in a god who created giant storms. They called this spirit *Hurakan*. European explorers who encountered these tremendous storms named them after the Indian god, but in English the spelling became *hurricane*.

Hurricanes destroyed many ships that European nations sent to the Americas. In the 1500s and 1600s, the great storms sank more than a hundred of the Spanish vessels that transported gold and silver between the New World and Spain.

EARLY HURRICANE RESEARCH

William Dampier, an English pirate, was one of the first people to discover a basic hurricane fact. Dampier's ship was caught in a hurricane in 1680 and blown about for hundreds of miles. Yet after the hurricane passed, Dampier was near the place where he had been when the storm had struck.

How could that be? A hurricane's winds move in a giant circle, Dampier concluded. He described a hurricane as a "vast whirlwind."

Some of the first efforts to warn people about approaching hurricanes came two centuries later. In the 1870s Father Benito Vines established a hurricane-warning system at Havana, Cuba. Father Vines took wind, temperature, and air pressure readings. He gathered reports from sailors and set up weather stations around the Caribbean. Whenever he concluded that a hurricane was on its way, the "Hurricane Priest" telegraphed warnings to islands of the West Indies and to the United States coast. His work inspired the United States to begin its own hurricane-warning system in 1898.

WHAT HURRICANES ARE AND HOW THEY WORK

Since Father Benito Vines' time, we have learned a great deal about hurricanes. Satellites that track hurricanes from space and special airplanes that fly into the storms have helped us gain this knowledge.

As William Dampier observed, hurricanes are giant windstorms that whirl in a circular motion. From space, hurricanes resemble pinwheels.

THE FIVE CATEGORIES OF HURRICANES

The Saffir-Simpson scale, below, is named for Robert Saffir, an engineer and expert on wind damage, and Dr. Bob Simpson, a hurricane expert. They wanted to be able to help officials determine the risks of an oncoming storm. Listed below are the wind speeds of each category. The complete scale also gives examples of the effects of the winds on buildings.

Winds From	Miles per Hour	Kilometers per Hour
Category One	74 to 95	119–153
Category Two	96–110	154–177
Category Three	111–130	178–209
Category Four	131–155	210–249
Category Five	155+	249+

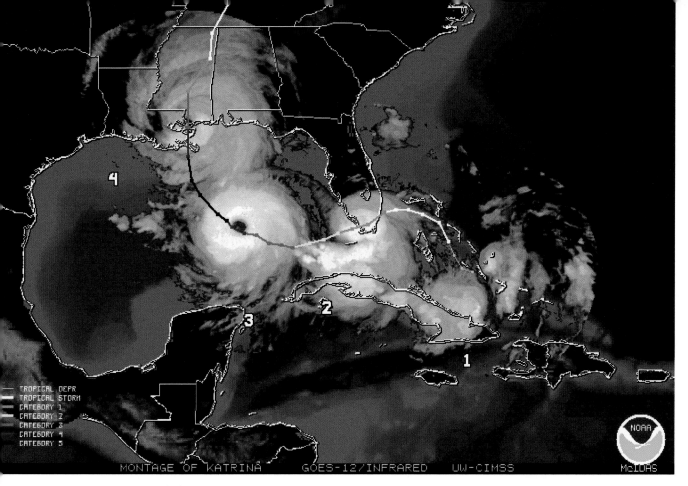

MONTAGE OF KATRINA   GOES-12/INFRARED   UW-CIMSS   McIDAS

This montage of NOAA images shows how Katrina developed into a monstrous storm over a period of days. 1 - mid-afternoon, August 23; 2 - early morning, August 26; 3 - early morning, August 28; 4 - morning, August 29, 2005.

A typical hurricane has a diameter of about 250 miles—about the size of Katrina. Hurricanes can travel thousands of miles and last several days. The maximum wind speeds in hurricanes are generally about 200 miles per hour—equal to the wind velocities of severe tornadoes.

Many of the hurricanes that strike the United States start out as *tropical waves* (not waves of water but weather disturbances) that come off Africa's western coast. Only about one tropical wave out of every ten gains enough power to become a hurricane. For that to occur, the tropical wave must organize into a rotating storm system called a *tropical depression*, with winds under 39 miles per hour. If it keeps strengthening and the winds reach 39 to 73 miles per hour, it then becomes a *tropical storm*. Tropical storms are given names, such as Tropical Storm Arlene or Tropical Storm Peter, off alphabetical lists. A wind speed of 74 miles per hour is the magic number. Should its winds reach that velocity, the storm officially becomes a hurricane.

"When the eye of the storm arrived the air was eerily still. In the distance, we could hear the roar of the wind. Then the hurricane winds arrived again, this time from the opposite direction. At daylight, I saw the 30-foot coconut palm tree in the front yard lying flat. Every mailbox on the street was on its side. Power lines were down. The power remained out for five days. Hurricane Cleo made me realize that I wanted to be a meteorologist."

Dennis Feltgen, describing a hurricane which struck Fort Lauderdale, Florida, in 1964 when he was 12 years old

A piece of plywood threaded into a tree trunk by 1992's Hurricane Andrew.

What people in North America call hurricanes have different names in other parts of the world: *typhoons* in the North Pacific Ocean and *tropical cyclones* in the Indian and South Pacific oceans. These giant storms that come off the sea also have local names. In Australia, for example, they are called *willy-willies*.

Each locale that is subject to such storms has a certain time of year when they are most likely to strike. Although there have been exceptions, the Atlantic hurricane season is often said to last from June 1 to November 30. Worldwide, May is the least active and September the most active month for the giant storms.

"The wind was the worst noise I have ever heard in my life. It sounded like a thousand freight trains and a thousand airplanes coming right at you. It was horrendous."

Richard I. Hadden, Pass Christian, Mississippi, describing Hurricane Camille of 1969

RECIPE FOR A HURRICANE

"Several factors must come together for a hurricane to form," explains Dennis Feltgen, a meteorologist (weather expert) with the National Oceanic and Atmospheric Administration (NOAA). Hurricane ingredients include ocean water, the sun's heat, air, wind, and the spin of the Earth.

The process of hurricane creation begins when the sun heats seawater. "Ocean waters of at least 80 degrees F through a depth of at least 150 feet" are required to begin hurricane formation, says Feltgen, which is why warm tropical waters are their spawning grounds.

"The sun-heated warm water evaporates and rises, cooling and forming clouds that head skyward," Feltgen continues. "If the air cools fast enough as it rises, it becomes unsettled, and showers and thunderstorms develop. This weather disturbance creates an area of low pressure that pulls in more and more warm, moist air." Given a twist by the Earth's spin, the growing storm begins to rotate. Spinning faster and faster as additional warm, moist air rushes in, the storm is pushed across the ocean by the wind. Despite the incredible fury within the hurricane, the entire storm moves forward slowly—at an average speed of 15 to 20 miles per hour.

There are several parts to a hurricane. The hurricane's *eye* is the center around which the powerful winds rotate. "The eye is an area of very light

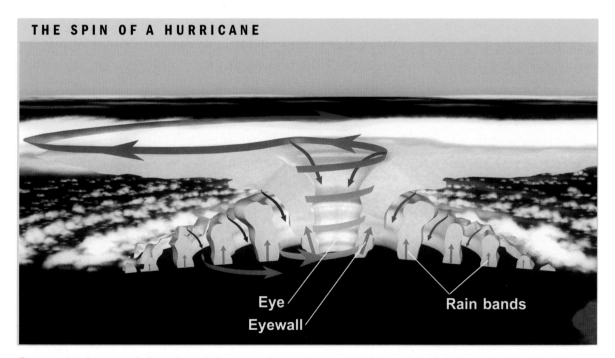

THE SPIN OF A HURRICANE

Eye
Eyewall
Rain bands

Because hurricanes spin in a giant circle, areas they pass over experience winds that keep changing direction. But hurricanes don't turn the same everywhere. Several forces combine to make them spin counterclockwise (opposite to the way a clock's hands move) in the Northern Hemisphere and clockwise (the same way a clock's hands move) in the Southern Hemisphere.

The aftereffects of Hurricane Rita's storm surge in 2005.

winds and a few clouds," says Scott Kiser, a hurricane expert with the National Weather Service. "In some cases you can see blue sky or, at night, the stars through the hurricane's eye. Surrounding a hurricane's eye are *eyewall clouds*. These towering clouds can be 10 miles high and most often produce the hurricane's strongest winds." Then there are the *spiral rain bands*. These are thunderstorm clouds. They are what give the hurricane its spiral shape.

The powerful winds of hurricanes have done some amazing things. They have yanked nails out of wood, driven pine needles deep into people's flesh, and toppled trains. By sending tree limbs flying and overturning cars and homes, hurricane winds have also been big killers.

Water, however, is by far the deadliest aspect of most hurricanes. The giant storms generate wind-driven walls of seawater called *storm surges* that flood coastal areas. Storm surges can reach heights of 30 feet—about as tall as a three-story building—and waves on top can make them still taller. These awesome walls of water account for most hurricane deaths that occur along seacoasts. Storm surges are somewhat similar to tsunamis, the giant waves created by earthquakes and volcanic eruptions that occur beneath or near the sea.

The outer rain bands of hurricanes can spin off waterspouts at sea and tornadoes over land.

Because they feed off warm ocean waters, hurricanes lose strength when they pass over land. Yet hurricanes (or *former* hurricanes, once their winds dip below 74 miles per hour) can still be deadly after moving inland. They can drop huge amounts of rain, causing inland flooding of streams and rivers far from the coast. "Allison in 2001 was a very weak tropical storm but it dumped lots of rain on Houston, Texas, causing $5 billion in damages," notes hurricane expert Scott Kiser. Because of their stormy conditions, hurricanes can also spin off deadly tornadoes. In 1967, Hurricane Beulah produced 115 tornadoes over Texas.

"Almost all hurricanes that make landfall spawn at least one tornado provided that enough of the hurricane's circulation moves over land."

Shirley Murillo, hurricane research meteorologist, NOAA

When a hurricane is especially devastating, its name is permanently retired and another name replaces it. There will never again be a Hurricane Katrina. On the alphabetical list of names that formerly included Katrina, the name Katia will be used instead.

In the next chapter, we will see how wind and water have done their deadly work in some famous hurricanes.

CHAPTER 3

"The Monstropolous
Beast"

Great Storms of History

Waves generated by the 1938
New England Hurricane crash
against a seawall.

"My God!...a total darkness above, the sea on fire, the wind roaring louder than thunder; the whole made more terrible by a very uncommon kind of blue lightning; the poor ship very much pressed, yet doing what she could, shaking her sides, and groaning at every stroke."

Lieutenant Archer, describing the wreck of the British ship *Phoenix* in a hurricane along Cuba in 1780

Hurricanes have destroyed cities and killed tens of thousands of people at a time. They have reshaped coastlines—and shaped history.

THE TYPHOONS THAT SAVED JAPAN: 1274 AND 1281

More than seven centuries ago, Kublai Khan ruled the Mongol Empire. This mighty empire included lands that are now China, Korea, and other parts of Asia. Kublai Khan might have also conquered Japan—if not for two typhoons.

In the fall of 1274, Kublai Khan sent 40,000 men in a thousand ships against Japan. They quickly conquered several Japanese strongholds and were winning a battle on the island of Kyushu when news of an approaching typhoon arrived. Hoping to get away before the storm hit, the invaders returned to their ships and headed out to sea. But they were too late. The typhoon struck the Mongol fleet with a fury. Three hundred ships sank or were wrecked along the Japanese coast, killing 13,000 invaders. Japan had been saved by a typhoon.

Seven years later, in the summer of 1281, Kublai Khan again attempted to conquer Japan, this time with 150,000 men in several thousand ships.

For six weeks the Japanese clashed with the invaders, but another typhoon decided the outcome. Once again the Mongol force tried but failed to evade the impending storm by heading out to sea. Four thousand vessels sank and 100,000 Mongol troops died in the typhoon. Although Kublai Khan's ship escaped, the Mongol emperor never again attacked Japan. Convinced that the gods had sent the storms to save them from the Mongols, the Japanese began calling a typhoon *kamikaze*—the "divine wind."

"A DREADFUL STORM AND HIDEOUS": ATLANTIC OCEAN, 1609

In 1607 English colonists founded Jamestown in what is now Virginia. They intended their settlement to be England's first permanent American colony. However, hunger and disease soon threatened to destroy the little community.

Help in the form of several ships carrying supplies and nearly 600 people sailed from England for Jamestown in the summer of 1609. En route they encountered a hurricane, which sank one vessel carrying 20 people. Other ships made it through the tempest to Jamestown, but the fleet's largest ship, the *Sea Venture*, never arrived. The vessel was presumed to have sunk in the hurricane.

In fact, the *Sea Venture* had been blown off course and wrecked off Bermuda, an uninhabited island 700 miles southeast of Jamestown. Its more than 100 passengers and crew scrambled onto dry land, where they found abundant fish to catch and berries to eat. One survivor, William Strachey, later wrote of the hurricane:

> "A dreadful storm and hideous began to blow, which swelling and roaring, did beat all light from heaven, which turned black upon us. The sea swelled above the clouds, and gave battle unto heaven. The water like whole rivers did flood the air."

Using the *Sea Venture's* remains, the castaways built two new ships. In the spring of 1610 they left Bermuda and once again headed to Jamestown, where the colonists had endured a disastrous winter. Of the settlement's 500 residents, only 60 were still alive.

Jamestown's remaining inhabitants were astonished when, in May of 1610, two little ships arrived with the long-missing castaways. The newcomers—and the supplies they brought—helped Jamestown survive to become England's first permanent American settlement. It was the seed of England's 13 colonies, which grew into the United States of America.

THE GALVESTON HURRICANE OF 1900

In 1900, Galveston had 38,000 people and was one of Texas's largest cities. With its beaches and warm ocean waters, Galveston was also a popular vacation spot.

Texas's "Queen City" had one drawback. Located two miles off the mainland on Galveston Island, it was a frequent target of hurricanes. Yet by 1900 little had been done to protect Galveston's people from sea storms.

On September 5 of that year U.S. Weather Bureau forecasters predicted that an approaching hurricane was a threat to Florida and other East Coast

> *"The mud! It is six inches thick over everything— a nasty, greasy, stinking stuff."*
>
> **Martin Nicholson**, describing the aftermath of the Galveston Hurricane of 1900

Because it was impossible to bury the thousands killed in the Galveston hurricane, most bodies were either burned or buried at sea.

locales. But the storm changed direction. Heading west toward Texas, it began to move into Galveston on the morning of September 8, 1900. Before people realized what was happening, buildings were being ripped apart by 140-mile-per-hour winds.

As in most hurricanes, water was the biggest killer. The storm surge and wind-whipped waves produced 20-foot walls of water, which picked up ships and lifted them out of Galveston's harbor. One vessel was carried onto the Texas mainland 22 miles from Galveston.

Houses, too, were washed away, drowning many people. Anna Delz, a girl who was thrown into the water when her home collapsed, was among those who survived. Holding onto a floating tree, then a roof, and then a large piece of wood, Anna wound up 18 miles from where her home had stood. Other people weren't as lucky. Arnold R. Wolfram described his experiences in Galveston following the great hurricane:

> *As I stepped off the sidewalk into the street, I stepped on something rather soft that gave way and nearly threw me down. I reached down under the water and discovered I had stepped on a dead woman. I turned away sick and horrified, but as I walked on, again and again, I saw bodies everywhere.*

By the time the hurricane moved out of Galveston late on September 8, at least 7,200 people had been killed in and near the city. The Galveston Hurricane of 1900 remains the deadliest natural disaster of any kind ever to strike the United States.

FLORIDA'S LAKE OKEECHOBEE HURRICANE OF 1928

Years ago some Americans called all the great storms "Florida hurricanes." That is because Florida, with its 1,350-mile coastline, has been battered by the most hurricanes of any state in the nation.

In September 1928 a hurricane with 150-mile-per-hour winds devastated the West Indies. The death toll in Puerto Rico was 1,500. The storm went on to strike Florida on September 16, claiming at least 26 lives around the coastal city of West Palm Beach.

"They saw other people like themselves struggling along. A house down, here and there, frightened cattle. But above all the drive of the wind and the water. Under its multiplied roar could be heard a mighty sound of grinding rock and timber and a wail. They looked back. Saw people trying to run in raging waters and screaming when they found they couldn't. The monstropolous beast [the lake] had left his bed. The two hundred miles an hour wind had loosed his chains. He rushed on, rolling the dikes, rolling the houses, rolling the people in the houses. The sea was walking the earth."

Zora Neale Hurston, describing the 1928 Lake Okeechobee Hurricane in her novel *Their Eyes Were Watching God*

Lake Okeechobee, as seen from space.

This hurricane remained strong while heading inland and still packed powerful winds when it reached southern Florida's 700-square-mile Lake Okeechobee. The winds piled up the lake's waters at its southern end. Hundreds of homes along the lakeshore were destroyed by the one-two punch of wind and water.

People who survived the collapse of their homes climbed trees to escape the floods. There some of them encountered another hazard: poisonous snakes called water moccasins also seeking shelter in the tree branches.

As many as 2,500 people around Lake Okeechobee perished in the 1928 hurricane. Years later farmers were still uncovering skeletal remains of the hurricane's victims.

THE NEW ENGLAND HURRICANE OF 1938

The southern and southeastern coasts aren't the only regions of the United States subject to hurricanes. This was tragically demonstrated in 1938 when a storm that appeared to be headed for Florida veered northward and hit the Northeast on September 21.

An estimated 2 billion trees were destroyed by the 1938 New England Hurricane.

"We could see the wave. It was forty feet high, just like a moving mountain."

Mae Higgins, survivor of the 1938 New England Hurricane

Its first target was the New Jersey coast, where wind and waves smashed houses and destroyed a bridge linking Atlantic City to an offshore island. On Long Island, New York, where several towns were demolished, the storm surge struck with such force that earthquake instruments 3,000 miles away detected the impact. Atop New York City's Empire State Building, wind gusts reached 120 miles per hour.

Farther up the coast, Rhode Island, the smallest of the country's 48 states, was hit hardest by the New England Hurricane. Many Rhode Islanders drowned as water destroyed seaside homes. Twelve feet of water flooded

Providence, the state's capital and largest city, completely submerging automobiles and forcing people to flee to higher floors in downtown buildings. Novelist F. Van Wyck Mason later described his experiences in Providence during the hurricane:

> Just as I got there, the roof of the [bus] station came off with a roar like a boiler factory. A woman seeking refuge on the top of her car was swept away before our eyes and drowned; there was nothing we could do. Another woman was wading to safety when she popped out of sight just like a jack-in-the-box; she evidently stepped into an open sewer. The lights of automobiles stayed on under the water, giving an eerie glow. Then the horns of automobiles all over the city short-circuited and kept up a deafening din all through the night.

The hurricane claimed dozens of additional victims in Massachusetts where, at one location, winds topped 180 miles per hour. By the time the New England Hurricane faded out in Canada on September 22, nearly 700 people had been killed and about 2,000 others had been severely injured.

HURRICANE CAMILLE: 1969

On August 17, 1969, a hurricane warning was broadcast over TV and radio informing Mississippi coastal residents that "extremely dangerous Camille" was coming their way. By evening, 100,000 Gulf Coast residents had fled inland. Some people didn't hear the warning, however. Others refused or were unable to leave their homes.

Hurricane Camille struck the Mississippi coast at about 9 P.M. Winds of up to 200 miles per hour and storm surges of up to 25 feet destroyed many buildings within a half mile of the ocean in several Mississippi communities. So powerful were the hurricane-driven waves that Ship Island off Biloxi, Mississippi, was actually cut in half. The two parts were later named East Ship Island and West Ship Island, and the body of water between the two became known as Camille Cut.

As houses toppled and floated away, there were many amazing stories of survival. Jacqueline and Leon Hines, who lived in Gulfport, Mississippi,

"I opened an upstairs bathroom window to look out, and the water was right at the level of the window—about 22 feet high. The bathroom was filling up higher and higher with water and the whole house was swaying from the water and the 190-mile-per-hour winds. I knew we had to get out of there. We had to go into that water."

Nancy Pryor Williams, who survived Hurricane Camille with her three children by clinging to floating debris

escaped the water by climbing up a 60-foot-tall outdoor TV antenna. "We had to climb higher and higher as the water rose," Jacqueline Hines later recalled. "I saw water go over the top of our house and then I couldn't even see the roof of our house. It was underwater." The couple was about halfway up the TV antenna when it broke off, throwing them into the water. Fortunately they made it to their roof, which was floating loose like a raft. There they remained until the waters subsided at 3:30 in the morning.

About 175 people along the Gulf Coast died. The weakening storm later dumped huge amounts of rain on the Virginia and West Virginia region, causing killer floods. Camille disappeared off the coast of Canada having taken about 325 lives in the United States.

EAST PAKISTAN CYCLONE: 1970

Tropical cyclones in the Bay of Bengal—an arm of the Indian Ocean off Asia—have claimed millions of lives over the centuries. In late 1970 a Bay of Bengal cyclone headed toward East Pakistan (now Bangladesh). The impoverished farming and fishing families in this storm's path received little warning. To make things worse, they lived in flimsy houses that were vulnerable to wind and water.

On the night of November 12–13, 1970, the cyclone slammed into the East Pakistan coast. Winds howling at 140 miles per hour awoke families sleeping in their huts. People who ran outside saw an enormous storm surge coming their way.

Some managed to survive by climbing palm trees, floating on bamboo poles, or even holding tightly to the tails of cattle. But the 20-foot wall of water was the last thing others saw. On one heavily populated offshore island the only creature to survive was a dog.

It is believed that the East Pakistan Cyclone of 1970 claimed more than 500,000 lives. It was the deadliest tropical cyclone, typhoon, or hurricane ever to occur, and killed more people than all the natural disasters ever to strike the United States added together.

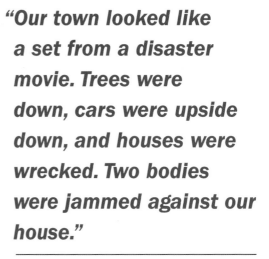

"Our town looked like a set from a disaster movie. Trees were down, cars were upside down, and houses were wrecked. Two bodies were jammed against our house."

Pat Maxwell of Long Beach, Mississippi, describing her town after Hurricane Camille struck in 1969

WITNESS TO A CYCLONE

"The force of the wave was terrible. It lifted me as I would lift one of my children. It was so dark I could not see, and because of the noise of the wind I could not hear. But I still had hold of my wife's hand and one of my children's hands. Then I was lifted and thrown hard against something solid. For a moment I was stunned. When I recovered I had my arms around a tree. But my hands were empty. I have not seen my wife or my eight children since."

A man named **Hussein**, who survived the East Pakistan Cyclone of 1970

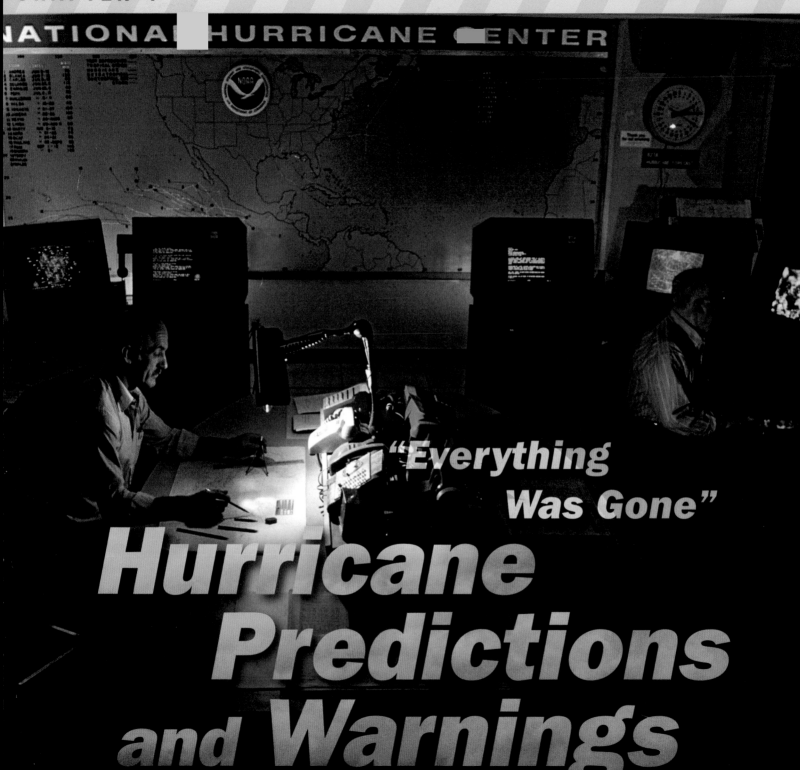

CHAPTER 4

NATIONAL HURRICANE CENTER

"Everything
Was Gone"

Hurricane
Predictions
and Warnings

Stormchaser George Kourounis measures the windspeed of Hurricane Dennis in Florida, 2005

**T**here is plenty to worry about concerning hurricanes.

The number of people at risk from the great storms has risen dramatically. By 2006 the number of Americans living in coastal counties facing the Atlantic Ocean or the Gulf of Mexico surpassed 60 million—equal to the nation's entire population back in 1890.

Adding to the danger is the fact that hurricanes have become more threatening. Katrina was just part of what made 2005 a horrendous hurricane year. The National Hurricane Center in Miami maintains a list of names for 21 possible tropical storms and hurricanes per year in the Atlantic Ocean and Gulf of Mexico. In 2005 there were a record 27 tropical storms and hurricanes—so many that every name on the list was used and six storms had to be designated with Greek letters.

"I saw the devastation from Katrina along the Mississippi coast. You could hardly tell where you were because everything was gone except the concrete slabs where buildings had stood....We drove for miles and it was all the same— nothing left."

Scott Kiser, National Weather Service hurricane expert

ATLANTIC HURRICANES OF 2005

NAME	STRONGEST WINDS	DATES
Tropical Storm Arlene	70 miles per hour	June 8–13
Tropical Storm Bret	40 m.p.h.	June 28–29
Hurricane Cindy	75 m.p.h.	July 3–7
Hurricane Dennis	150 m.p.h.	July 4–13
Hurricane Emily	160 m.p.h.	July 10–21
Tropical Storm Franklin	70 m.p.h.	July 21–29
Tropical Storm Gert	40 m.p.h.	July 23–25
Tropical Storm Harvey	65 m.p.h.	August 2–8
Hurricane Irene	100 m.p.h.	August 4–18
Tropical Storm José	50 m.p.h.	August 22–23
Hurricane Katrina	175 m.p.h.	August 23–31
Tropical Storm Lee	40 m.p.h.	August 28–September 2
Hurricane Maria	115 m.p.h.	September 1–10
Hurricane Nate	90 m.p.h.	September 5–10
Hurricane Ophelia	85 m.p.h.	September 6–18
Hurricane Philippe	80 m.p.h.	September 17–24
Hurricane Rita	175 m.p.h.	September 17–26
Hurricane Stan	80 m.p.h.	October 1–5
Tropical Storm Tammy	50 m.p.h.	October 5–6
Hurricane Vince	75 m.p.h.	October 9–11
Hurricane Wilma	185 m.p.h.	October 15–25
Tropical Storm Alpha	50 m.p.h.	October 22–24
Hurricane Beta	115 m.p.h.	October 27–31
Tropical Storm Gamma	45 m.p.h.	November 18–21
Tropical Storm Delta	70 m.p.h.	November 23–28
Hurricane Epsilon	75 m.p.h.	November 29–December 8
Tropical Storm Zeta	65 m.p.h.	December 29–January 6, 2006

Raging flood waters in the wake of Hurricane Stan, 2005, destroyed train tracks and a bridge in Chiapas, a state in Mexico.

Besides producing the most named storms, 2005 set many other records. The most hurricanes in a single year had been 12 in 1969. That record fell in 2005, which had 15. The most Category 5 hurricanes in a year had been two, which occurred in both 1960 and 1961. A new record was set in 2005, which had four Category 5 hurricanes: Emily, Katrina, Rita, and Wilma. Furthermore, of the six strongest hurricanes on record, three of them— Wilma, Rita, and Katrina—occurred in 2005.

The record number of major hurricanes to strike U.S. shores in a year had been three, which occurred most recently in 2004. This mark was also blown away in 2005, when four major hurricanes—Dennis, Katrina, Rita, and Wilma—hit the United States. Together, the years 2003, 2004, and 2005 had 30 hurricanes. Previously, the most hurricanes in a three-year period had been 27, in 1886–1888.

In fact, since 1995 we have been in a period of especially numerous and powerful hurricanes, explains meteorologist Scott Kiser. It appears that periods of intense hurricane activity occur naturally at times due to cyclical changes in the oceans and atmosphere that are not yet understood.

"The 1950s and '60s also brought a period of high hurricane activity," says Kiser. "For example, Hurricane Carla in 1961 was so large the storm's clouds covered the Gulf of Mexico. That hurricane produced wind gusts to 170 miles per hour along the central Texas coast. Hurricane Betsy in 1965 was the first storm to cause a billion dollars' worth of damage. It produced winds of 125 miles per hour in New Orleans. The storm caused water to overflow the levees and flooded the city in some locations up to the roofs."

Many scientists also believe that by polluting our planet's atmosphere, human beings are contributing to the increase in hurricane activity.

When we burn automobile gasoline, oil, natural gas, and coal, huge quantities of carbon dioxide gas (CO_2) are released into the atmosphere. Over the past two centuries, the amount of CO_2 in the atmosphere has greatly increased. The CO_2 traps heat that would otherwise escape into space, thus warming our planet. Other pollutants we produce also block heat from escaping. The result is known as global warming. Temperatures on our planet have climbed by an average of one degree Fahrenheit over the past century. They may increase by several more degrees in the 21st century.

The oceans have warmed along with the rest of the Earth. Studies reveal that the top 1,000 feet of the oceans are half a degree Fahrenheit warmer today than they were 50 years ago. Since hurricanes are fueled by warm ocean waters, many scientists believe that the 21st century will continue to have much more powerful hurricanes than those of the past and perhaps larger numbers of the great storms.

Fortunately, there is also some good news. Over the past few decades we have improved our ability to predict when and where storms will strike. Weather agencies in all parts of the world now carefully track hurricanes, typhoons, and tropical cyclones. Many nations besides the United States, including Mexico, Japan, China, Australia, India, Thailand, Korea, and Indonesia, have systems to monitor and warn people about approaching giant storms.

Boats piled up after Hurricane Hugo hit the barrier island of Isle of Palms, South Carolina, in 1989.

"*Rain streaks the windows as we fly over the first few bumps. Anticipation grows as the pilot steers the plane into the storm's strongest winds in the eyewall. Updrafts and downdrafts bounce the airplane around. We are wearing seat belts and shoulder harnesses, but at one point the plane bounces around so much that I sit on my hands to keep them from flailing around. Thick clouds darken the cabin. We measure a wind gust of 150 miles per hour. Then, after the last bump, we punch through the wall of clouds and sunshine fills the hurricane's eye. The winds are light, the sun is shining, and there is blue sky above the clouds that tower around the plane. It makes me feel like a small ant at the bottom of a cereal bowl looking up at the clouds all around the eye.*"

Meteorologist **Dick Fletcher**, recalling a flight with the NOAA Hurricane Hunters into the eye of Hurricane Diana in 1984

A Hurricane Hunter aircraft, specially equipped to fly into hurricanes, gather data, and safely bring the crew and scientists back to land.

Weather satellites in space are the main tool for monitoring storms at sea. The first satellite to transmit detailed weather pictures back to Earth was Tiros I, launched by the United States in 1960. Since then, the U.S., Japan, and European nations have launched numerous weather satellites that provide images and data concerning the movement, size, and strength of ocean storms.

Radar is another valuable tool in widespread use. Radar signals bounce off raindrops in the sky, revealing information about the moisture in hurricanes. The United States also sends airplane crews called Hurricane Hunters into the giant storms. The Hurricane Hunters actually fly into the eyes of hurricanes to gather data about the storms. Although the airplane rides can be bumpy, information the Hurricane Hunters gather about a storm helps scientists predict what might happen next.

For storms threatening the United States, scientists at the National Hurricane Center in Miami study the information gathered by weather satellites, aircraft, and radar. With the help of computers they determine where and how hard a hurricane is likely to strike. If National Hurricane Center forecasters conclude that a hurricane may slam into a coastal region within the next 36 hours, they issue a hurricane watch. Because hurricanes can change direction, a *hurricane watch* is issued for a bigger region than may actually be hit by the storm. People who live in a coastal region that comes under a hurricane watch should

- *Pay close attention to further instructions that may be broadcast over TV and radio.*

- *Make sure they have a means of escape; people who don't have a car must arrange to leave the area by some other means.*

- *Plan an escape route; in almost every case it is best to head away from the ocean.*

- *Make sure to have fresh drinking water and other emergency supplies.*

- *Be prepared to board up windows and secure outdoor belongings such as boats and lawn furniture; besides protecting these items, this may prevent them from being turned into deadly missiles by the wind.*

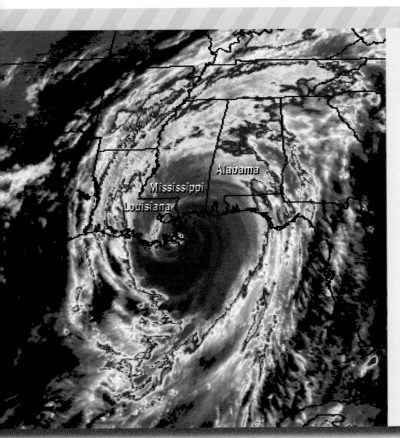

"I've flown into numerous hurricanes with the Hurricane Hunters, the most recent one being Hurricane Rita in 2005. We drop an instrument called the GPSdropwindsonde from the aircraft that travels down through the storm. It collects measurements of wind speed, wind direction, air temperature, relative humidity, and pressure every half second. After reviewing the data for any errors, I transmit it via satellite to the National Hurricane Center. From the data we can tell if the storm is weakening or intensifying and make computer weather models to better forecast the storm track and intensity."

Shirley Murillo, hurricane research meteorologist, NOAA

If the hurricane watch changes to a *hurricane warning,* the situation has become an emergency. A hurricane warning means that a hurricane is actually expected to strike a region within the next 24 hours. People in the warned area should

- *Flee the moment officials advise this course of action; they should head inland or go to a local storm shelter if that is what officials recommend.*

- *Make sure all people and pets are indoors if for some reason they must remain at home through the storm.*

- *If at home, continue to listen to weather bulletins and stay away from windows.*

It must be remembered that a hurricane can cause floods far inland. People near an inland river or stream that tends to flood may have to flee if a hurricane or its remnants approaches.

Typhoon Haitang, in 2005, brings strong winds and heavy rains to a province in China.

Amid all the confusion that a hurricane can create, there is one thing above all to keep in mind. Father Luis Aponte-Merced, who survived Hurricane Katrina, expressed it simply and well:

Don't ignore hurricane warnings. Any time it's said a hurricane will occur, take it seriously and, if at all possible, get out of the danger area—ahead of time.

"In the eye of a hurricane, you learn things other than of a scientific nature. You feel the puniness of man and his works."

Newscaster Edward R. Murrow, with the Hurricane Hunters in the eye of Hurricane Edna in 1954

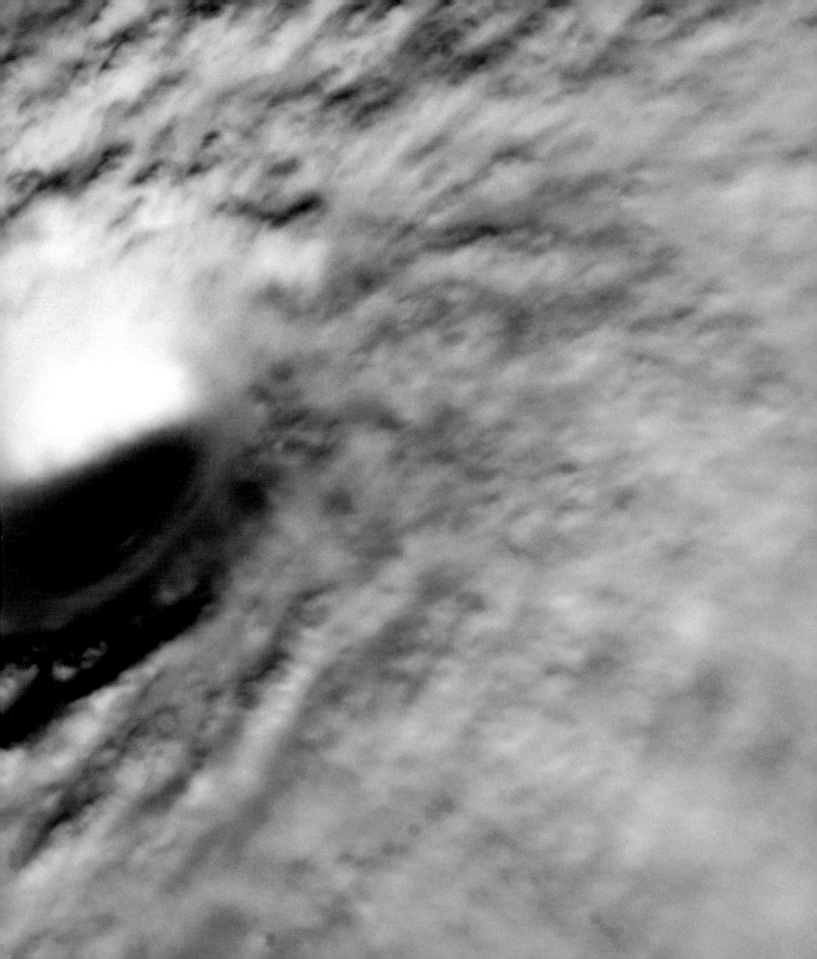

Glossary

air pressure (or atmospheric pressure)—pressure caused by the weight of the air; hurricanes form from low-pressure systems and the air pressure in a hurricane's eye tends to be extremely low

atmosphere—the gases surrounding a heavenly body; what we on Earth commonly call "air"

climate—the typical weather a region has exhibited over many years

clockwise—the same way a clock's hands move

coast—the land along a large body of water

counterclockwise—opposite to the way a clock's hands move

cycles—events that occur at fairly regular intervals

evacuate—to leave an area for safety reasons

evaporation—the process by which water is converted into water vapor or "dried up"

eye (of a hurricane)—the calm center of a hurricane

eyewall clouds (or wall clouds)—the

This man holds a hurricane ball, one of nature's oddities. Plant debris swirled by wind-driven waters sometimes takes the shape of a tightly woven ball.

storm clouds near the eye that produce a hurricane's strongest winds and heaviest rains

forecaster (of weather)—a person who studies data and predicts future weather conditions

global warming—the theory that air pollution is raising Earth's temperature, which may result in unusual weather including much more powerful hurricanes than in the past

hurricane—a huge windstorm with winds of at least 74 miles per hour whirling in a giant circle

hurricane warning—a weather bulletin warning people that a hurricane is expected to strike a specific coastal area within the next 24 hours

hurricane watch—a weather bulletin informing people in a coastal region that a hurricane may strike within 36 hours

inland—away from the seacoast and toward the interior

inland flood—a flood, sometimes caused by rain from hurricanes, that occurs some distance from the seacoast

levees—natural or man-made walls that prevent rivers and lakes from flooding the land

meteorologist—a weather scientist

pollution—the conditions produced when we dirty our planet's air, water, and land

radar—an instrument that can detect and study distant objects by means of reflected radio waves; weather monitoring is one of its uses

spiral rain bands— the part of a hurricane that gives it its distinctive pinwheel shape; the bands are thunderstorm clouds

storm shelter—a structure built to withstand storms and to serve as a place of safety during storms

storm surge—wind-driven wall of seawater

tornado—violently whirling column of air that descends from thundercloud systems and touches ground; it can be produced by hurricanes

tropical cyclone—the name for a hurricane in the Indian Ocean or the South Pacific Ocean

tropical depression—a storm system over tropical seas with winds whirling at less than 39 miles per hour

tropical storm—a storm system with whirling winds of at least 39 but less than 74 miles per hour

tropical waves—weather disturbances in the tropics that can be an early stage of hurricane development

tropics—regions of the Earth known for their warm climate located within about 1,600 miles north or south of the equator

typhoon—the name for a hurricane in the North Pacific Ocean

weather—conditions of the air including such factors as wind, heat, and moisture

weather satellites—spacecraft, orbiting Earth, that monitor our world's weather

whirlwind—a rotating windstorm

Bibliography

BOOKS

Allen, Everett S. *A Wind to Shake the World: The Story of the 1938 Hurricane*. Boston: Little, Brown, 1976.

Barnes, Jay. *Florida's Hurricane History*. Chapel Hill: University of North Carolina Press, 1998.

Best, Gary Dean. *FDR and the Bonus Marchers, 1933–1935*. Westport, Connecticut: Praeger, 1992.

Bixel, Patricia Bellis, and Elizabeth Hayes Turner. *Galveston and the 1900 Storm*. Austin: University of Texas Press, 2000.

Davies, Pete. *Inside the Hurricane: Face to Face with Nature's Deadliest Storms*. New York: Holt, 2000.

Douglas, Marjory Stoneman. *Hurricane*. New York: Rinehart, 1958.

Emanuel, Kerry. *Divine Wind: The History and Science of Hurricanes*. New York: Oxford University Press, 2005.

Greene, Casey Edward, and Shelly Henley Kelly, editors. *Through a Night of Horrors: Voices from the 1900 Galveston Storm*. College Station: Texas A&M University Press, 2000.

Moraes, Dom. *The Tempest Within: An Account of East Pakistan*. London: Vikas Publications, 1971.

Rosenfeld, Jeffrey. *Eye of the Storm: Inside the World's Deadliest Hurricanes, Tornadoes, and Blizzards*. New York: Plenum, 1999.

Sheets, Bob, and Jack Williams. *Hurricane Watch: Forecasting the Deadliest Storms on Earth*. New York: Vintage Books, 2001.

Countless numbers of pets and animals were lost during Hurricane Katrina. This lucky dog found a dry roof to wait for rescue.

Further Reading and Research

FOR FURTHER READING

Gaffney, Timothy R. *Hurricane Hunters*. Berkeley Heights, New Jersey: Enslow, 2001.

Meister, Cari. *Hurricanes*. Edina, Minnesota: ABDO, 1999.

Nicolson, Cynthia Pratt. *Hurricane!* Toronto, Ontario, Canada: Kids Can Press, 2002.

Richards, Julie. *Howling Hurricanes*. Broomall, Pennsylvania: Chelsea House, 2002.

Simon, Seymour. *Hurricanes*. New York: HarperCollins, 2003.

Souza, D.M. *Hurricanes*. Minneapolis, Minnesota: Carolrhoda, 1996.

Steele, Christy. *Hurricanes*. Austin, Texas: Steadwell, 2000.

WEBSITES TO EXPLORE

Home page of the National Hurricane Center/ Tropical Prediction Center website, with links to many fascinating pages about hurricanes:

http://www.nhc.noaa.gov/

Home page of the Air Force Reserve's Hurricane Hunters with links to photos, stories, and information on specific storms:

http://www.hurricanehunters.com/

Home page of a Hurricane Hunter's photo album:

http://home.att.net/~typhoon1/index.html

Home page of the University of Illinois Hurricane Online Meteorology Guide, with links on such subjects as the structure of hurricanes and a global perspective:

http://ww2010.atmos.uiuc.edu/(Gh)/guides/ mtr/hurr/home.rxml

NASA website on hurricanes:

http://kids.earth.nasa.gov/archive/hurricane/ index.html

National Geographic website focusing on hurricanes and other types of natural disasters:

http://www.nationalgeographic.com/eye/ natures.html

Interviews by the Authors

Father Luis Aponte-Merced, O.F.M., Peoria, Illinois

Dennis Feltgen, NOAA meteorologist, Silver Spring, Maryland

Dick Fletcher, chief meteorologist, WTSP-TV, Tampa/St. Petersburg, Florida

Richard I. Hadden, Pass Christian, Mississippi

Jake Herty III, hydrometeorological technician, National Weather Service forecast office, Slidell, Louisiana

Jacqueline and Leon Hines, Gulfport, Mississippi

Scott Kiser, National Weather Service meteorologist and hurricane expert, Silver Spring, Maryland

Major Philip Kitchen, Orleans Parish Civil Sheriff's Office

Pat Maxwell, Long Beach, Mississippi

George Michael Mixon, Pass Christian, Mississippi

Shirley Murillo, hurricane research meteorologist, NOAA, Miami, Florida

Ceyonne Riley, Houston, Texas

Lance Williams, Houston, Texas

Nancy Pryor Williams, Pass Christian, Mississippi

Hurricane Frances blew through a Florida grapefruit grove in 2004.

Acknowledgments

The authors thank **Dennis Feltgen**, NOAA meteorologist, Silver Spring, Maryland, for reviewing portions of the manuscript. Dennis grew up in South Florida, experiencing several hurricanes in the 1960s. He graduated from Florida State University in 1974 with a Bachelor of Science degree in Meteorology. He spent nearly 30 years as a television reporter and meteorologist, giving live reports from hurricanes during the 1980s and 1990s. He joined NOAA in 2002, spending three years in Key West, Florida, forecasting the effects of a dozen hurricanes to threaten or strike the Keys, including 2005's Dennis, Katrina, and Rita. He joined NOAA National Weather Service Public Affairs in 2005.

Thanks also to **Scott Kiser**, National Weather Service (NWS) meteorologist and hurricane expert, Silver Spring, Maryland, for answering several scientific questions. Scott grew up in southeast Texas near the Gulf of Mexico coast where hurricanes were a threat every year. He stayed in Texas for his college education, studying at North Texas State University and Texas A & M University. Even after 32 years with the NWS Scott's love of weather continues. He is married with two grown children.

Finally, thanks to **Shirley Murillo**, NOAA hurricane research meteorologist, Miami, Florida. Shirley began her career while she was in a senior in high school, working as an intern at NOAA's Hurricane Research Division in Miami. As she says, "I became interested in weather when I was young. When Hurricane Andrew (1992) made landfall in Miami. I was amazed at its strength and damage that occurred. This experience made me want to study hurricanes and help improve our understanding."

Shirley gets to fly into hurricanes in specially equipped aircraft as part of her job. Otherwise, she's on the ground collecting information. In her spare time, she is busy with family, friends and her dog Heidi.

If you have a question about hurricanes, or if you want to talk about hurricanes, feel free to contact the authors. Dennis and Judy can be reached at: fradinbooks@comcast.net

Index